*For Justin, Jonathan, Joshua, Jacob, Clark, Harrison,
Claire, Ben, Andy, Christian, Reed, Andrew, Matthew,
Annabelle, Addie, and Skyler*
H. F.

For every new life, and for Kathe
R. L.

Wake Up!

poem by
Helen Frost

photographs by
Rick Lieder

CANDLEWICK PRESS

Sun says, Wake up—
come out and explore.

New life is exploding
outside your door!

What's new in the sky?

What's going on in the trees?

Who's inside these eggs?

What catches
the breeze?

New life is everywhere—

open your eyes.

That might be an ant—
but look—
it flies!

At the edge of the pond,
where frogs croak and kiss,

look into the water—
what is this?

Whose baby hides
in the forest?

Which twins are
born on a farm?

Who breaks out of an eggshell
and snuggles, close and warm?

So many new creatures
with so much to do—

the world is
wide awake.

Are you?

Sunlight shines through translucent eggs that will soon become **gray garden slugs.**

A newly hatched **Chinese praying mantis** steps across an **English daisy.**

A **tree swallow** flies back to its nest with an insect for its hungry babies.

Four **tree swallow** eggs have been laid in a nest lined with soft feathers.

Dandelion seeds land in a patch of wild **violets** and float away on the breeze.

This tadpole lives in the water as it grows into a **red-eyed tree frog.**

White-tailed deer babies, called fawns, have white spots, which makes them harder to see in dappled sunlight on a forest floor.

These lambs, the babies of **domestic sheep,** were born within minutes of each other. They are just a few hours old.

A hatching **mute swan** is pecking a hole in its shell.

A **sandhill crane** chick, about a week old, goes exploring.

Baby **American robins** open their beaks as they wait for their parents to feed them.

A **vinegar fly** lands on a blade of grass and faces a **sawfly** larva.

Mating pairs of two different kinds of birds, **great blue herons** and **great white egrets,** bring sticks and build nests at the top of a tree.

Newly hatched **cellar spiders** walk near their father on a blade of grass.

A **Chinese praying mantis** casts a shadow on the petal of a **peony.**

Most ants do not fly, but each colony has one queen ant who is the mother of all the other ants in the colony. This is a **winter ant** queen and she can fly.

These **green frogs** will mate and their eggs will hatch into tadpoles.

A newly hatched **mute swan,** called a cygnet, is still wet as it stays close to the other cygnets who hatched before it.

A family of **woodchucks** comes out from under a bridge into the sunlight.

A **common grackle,** not quite ready to leave the nest, calls out for food.

A **European honeybee** carries pollen from one flower to another.

Library of Congress Catalog Card Number pending. ISBN 978-0-7636-8149-4. This book was typeset in Cygnet.

Candlewick Press, 99 Dover Street, Somerville, Massachusetts 02144. visit us at www.candlewick.com.

Printed in Shenzhen, Guangdong, China. 16 17 18 19 20 21 CCP 10 9 8 7 6 5 4 3 2 1

FSC
MIX
Paper from responsible sources
www.fsc.org FSC® C008047